THE PORTAGE POETRY SERIES

I0517728

SERIES TITLES

The Coronation of the Ghost
Benjamin Gantcher

The Stone Tries to Understand the Hands
Susannah Sheffer

Red Camaro
Dwaine Rieves

Where Babies Come From
Ori Fienberg

Cuttings
Hannah Dow

Forgive the Animal
Sarah Pape

Love as Invasive Species
Ellen Kombiyil

They Were Horrible Cooks
Allison Whittenberg

The New Life
Wendy Wisner

Restoring Prairie
Margaret Rozga

Table with Burning Candle
Julia Paul

A Bright Wound
Sarah A. Etlinger

The Velvet Book
Rae Gouirand

Listening to Mars
Sally Ashton

Glitter City
Bonnie Jill Emanuel

The Trouble with Being a Childless Only Child
Michelle Meyer

Happy Everything
Caitlin Cowan

Dear Lo
Brady Bove

Sadness of the Apex Predator
Dion O'Reilly

Do Not Feed the Animal
Hikari Miya

The Watching Sky
Judy Brackett Crowe

Let It Be Told in a Single Breath
Russell Thorburn

The Blue Divide
Linda Nemec Foster

Lake, River, Mountain
Mark B. Hamilton

Talking Diamonds
Linda Nemec Foster

Poetic People Power
Tara Bracco (ed.)

The Green Vault Heist
David Salner

There is a Corner of Someplace Else
Camden Michael Jones

Everything Waits
Jonathan Graham

We Are Reckless
Christy Prahl

Always a Body
Molly Fuller

Bowed As If Laden With Snow
Megan Wildhood

Silent Letter
Gail Hanlon

New Wilderness
Jenifer DeBellis

Fulgurite
Catherine Kyle

The Body Is Burden and Delight
Sharon White

Bone Country
Linda Nemec Foster

Not Just the Fire
R.B. Simon

Monarch
Heather Bourbeau

The Walk to Cefalù
Lynne Viti

The Found Object Imagines a Life: New and Selected Poems
Mary Catherine Harper

Naming the Ghost
Emily Hockaday

Mourning
Dokubo Melford Goodhead

Messengers of the Gods: New and Selected Poems
Kathryn Gahl

After the 8-Ball
Colleen Alles

Careful Cartography
Devon Bohm

Broken On the Wheel
Barbara Costas-Biggs

Sparks and Disperses
Cathleen Cohen

Holding My Selves Together: New and Selected Poems
Margaret Rozga

Lost and Found Departments
Heather Dubrow

Marginal Notes
Alfonso Brezmes

The Almost-Children
Cassondra Windwalker

Meditations of a Beast
Kristine Ong Muslim

PRAISE FOR

The Coronation of the Ghost

"Dying in the Late Anthropocene/the graveyard washed out and power down/ no way to complete the cremation" Ben Gantcher writes in his stunning book *The Coronation of the Ghost*. Andre Breton urged 'the recovery of our psychic forces' by 'a dizzying descent into ourselves.' In his new work Gantcher takes a turn for the wild. He's forging a surrealism for the twenty-first century, incandescent with the exploratory zing of the forerunners, but free of their rhetorical self-belief. Gantcher's poems confront the end of language. They know every path we have leads to the abyss. They find their own way trope by trope, vulnerable, rueful, autonomous: 'outside of ourselves, what certainties are left.' Poems examine themselves for a way out: 'I want to know if boarding the last transport / to summer's hidden inside the word burgeon.' The entire book shape-shifts beyond the template of text, because it's late and the need is terrifying—and aren't we and our books ghosts already? Visceral, humane, contrarian, often wildly funny or bracingly matter-of-fact, *The Coronation of the Ghost* is brilliant."

—D. NURKSE
author of *A Country of Strangers*

"Reading as Benjamin Gantcher puts all his heart and energy into imagining what holds the world together, I hear a sound like a song played by bees on a piano left out in the street in the rain—a music the notes of which land 'on the very / it seems nearly / late down beat.' That beautiful tune will stay in your head, making you attend to, struggle with, and marvel at the glittering, the highway, the lantern fly, the irate narrator. It means everything it is supposed to mean and it is so satisfying. Long live this Ghost!"

—JORDAN DAVIS
author of *Shell Game*

"Ben Gantcher's magisterial *The Coronation of the Ghost*, heir to New York school colloquy and Ashbery's antic surreal, navigates deftly (by train, car, bike, and foot, in the ambulatory Romantic tradition) between noise and music, technocracy and nature, and meaning and its annihilation, in poems that bespeak both the sublimity and alienation of the Anthropocene. With tenderness, wit, and verve, Gantcher distills moments worth cherishing in a haunted landscape of simulacrum, bar codes, apps, and smokestacks, bringing to the reader a 'rabbit hour' of contemplation and eros. An ungraspable feminine presence pervades the collection, along with exclamations and questions of great urgency ('Will seedtime lead to harvest? Outside ourselves, what certainties are left?'), and in its coronation of the king of ghosts, one senses that only Gantcher has the moral resolve and lyrical gifts to complete this journey into, and out of, an abyssal underworld of our design. These impassioned, ingenious soliloquies are what Hamlet would have written, had he not gone mad, and had Gantcher's profound gift of negative capability. The pathos of this book inheres in Gantcher's refusal to close the door on others—including nature, ghosts, spirits, and the dead—and in his exacting, bravura animation of these 'voices / of the non-human world' we delight, becalmed, knowing that a poet of our time has made a way for us, and a 'keyhole of instructive light.'"

—VIRGINIA KONCHAN
author of *Requiem*

"Ben Gantcher's poems are located in a distinctly urban landscape that is at the same time a riotous natural habitat—because of course; that's how it is. These poems toggle back and forth so deftly between registers—high and low, urban and natural, plainspoken and formal. The cacophony feels and sounds like riding the subway, and like riding the subway, these poems keep you guessing, keep you on your toes. The sheer range of THINGS in these poems makes each page a little cabinet of wonders."

—MATTHEW ROHRER
author of *Army of Giants*

The Coronation of the Ghost

Benjamin Gantcher

CORNERSTONE PRESS
UNIVERSITY OF WISCONSIN-STEVENS POINT

Cornerstone Press, Stevens Point, Wisconsin 54481
Copyright © 2025 Benjamin Gantcher

www.uwsp.edu/cornerstone

Printed in the United States of America by
Point Print and Design Studio, Stevens Point, Wisconsin

Library of Congress Control Number: 2024947477
ISBN: 978-1-960329-58-5

Artwork in "The Romance of the Fittest" Copyright © 2023 Alexis Myre
Artwork in "Rendez-Vous with the Revelator" Copyright © 2023 Michael Aaron Lee
Artwork in "Sparrows" Copyright © 2024 Nils Folke Anderson

Cornerstone Press titles are produced in courses and internships offered by the
Department of English at the University of Wisconsin–Stevens Point.

DIRECTOR & PUBLISHER
Dr. Ross K. Tangedal

EXECUTIVE EDITORS
Jeff Snowbarger, Freesia McKee

EDITORIAL DIRECTOR
Ellie Atkinson

SENIOR EDITORS
Brett Hill, Grace Dahl

PRESS STAFF
Carolyn Czerwinski, Elyse Edens, Sophie McPherson, Kylie Newton, Ava Willett

To Miles, Leo, and May

ALSO BY BENJAMIN GANTCHER:

Snow Farmer

Strings of Math and Custom

CONTENTS

Misterioso

Echelons of Spring

My mother had said, "…do you ever feel that you have died and are walking among those who might have died as well but are not telling?

"Because," my mother said, "no one tells."

—Joy Williams

Not a ghost but

would be embraced

—William Carlos Williams

Misterioso

Come On Up to the House

I boarded the J with hope of becoming a red balloon.
The condos, embarrassed, stopped at the bridge, panting.
I flew solitary among the isolates
over the silvers of the river that are moments and generations.
Where those emissaries of the moon, the pigeons, take the sun,
on the dream-long battened hut like a teahouse with poor service,
I accepted the descent like opening a skin. You were with me
as you'd always been, fate having drawn
the map in fits and lunges,
so that when, as we crossed
Saratoga for the gate where the drunks
play chess, the yellow light woke up, the sign to hurry,
your hackles went up, and up top the lightning
gray switches were freaking out in pure joy
as if the dead were reaching through the iron corduroy
lindens
to exult in the heaven that pelted us
with legions of disputatious commentaries on the impulse to read
every gesture, and those were sizzling.
As if arthritic praise broke past the unpacked bedrooms
and took on the disoriented.
Where the rabbits might have been—it was the rabbit hour
when the edges go soft and it's safe
for those children of the world to abandon the borders—
had there been rabbits, there was space, if I could set down
beside you, but all that prayer was a wind that with the toes of my shoes
drew rings and rings in rings.

In the Beginning

On that fateful day,
same as any day,
as if my soul had gotten its mitts
on a box of cassettes

and unspooled a confusion
of mixtapes in the Kentucky
coffee tree, the sun was scribbling
the bronze-black glimmering

fish, illegibly
eloquent, and printing music
on the sidewalk where the dry
cleaner smoothed it with her broom.

As if *sub rosa*,
sort of davening,
the two of us, skirt
for ticket, take heart,

she and I giving
the other the slip, and windmill
round the broom in a tango
of limbs and echoes.

Bushwick Yellow

Louder out here under the el
than *trestle*, the sun considering
seriously the virtue of sunflowers
at the Dollar. What if monkeys
that clash cymbals were how
the sun dreams of us, were
how you dream of me?
The glad waxy silk sunflowers
are text and inspiration. Sunday,
their tramps will come. *The Fire
of Love* sticks with you, the Foley
of lava in your ear, the animated prints
and maps of volcanoes like the light-
industrial district
emptied of people
I stick to so I
can love people. The folly
of the princess sunflowers
and the clownish bee.

Sheila

It's early rush hour. The puffy
coats in soot and solemnity
find room to mushroom
and make inadvertent snake
love. The train
creaks like timber and gets stuck
in the tunnel
again. Signal
problems with my phone too. The
car is
pine needles have fallen
quiet. In the dark
a landslide carries off
a pterodactyl and
we rest
fitfully until a nurse
with cell service gathers us
in her kitchen
talking about
Sheila this

Misterioso

You ride the wrong way on the block,
peddling into the citrus
spackling with a beelike *mm-hm* on the very
it seems nearly
late down beat and lift
off into the proliferant
letters of sun and plane
tree, a full-body scholar
at the ur card catalogue, like the bee
that grapples on the bee
balm were a marmoreal hand
to have picked out notes
on a rained-on upright
and they sprouted in the wardrobe
that I planted on the steps
pollen and blush
purple and chartreuse
stuck and stravaging, jurisdictions of sprung
sky placed up the
cliff-face at Chauvet
and me hearing the street's smudging
of the crimson and gold of your ride.

In the porches of the ear,

anxiously watching
a pianist like forgiven Arachne pick out
where to place the lucent affections along a wing
of the austerities
I mean pretty out of it in the cold
doctor's office, at the most animate
a seed, I was wakened by a tremor
and bam, the boys, storm and thunder,
go at the text
with a femur and tongs.
They flank the stroller
and the mom, a fully charged
vortex between the benjamin
bush and the desk.
She was furious and dared us
and I looked unwelcomely
curious about the slow trip in the tight
elevator so that I felt
the source of an age old
awe and slyly
shared of her.

My Neighbor, Pipilotti Rist

Orange streak
the fat pit bull wriggles up
the stoop to sniff
is it pee-stained that frippery of winter
cabbages? the shriveled
licorice with caked
talc as if bewigged
lords had deliquesced
down the steps
she squats
beside a creased
War and Peace and
castoff xmas
baubles—relief
under the hallelujah
chorus, the leaves
on the concrete like last
year's applause
(I foraged
a tape of *Twin Peaks*!)
And this and more is the poem
she sees
on the indigo
slubsilk video.

What Did You Think It Was About?

With all the light that sprays out of us
it follows that those lab techs, my
kids, register the scattering
data and assemble my life
like an unzipped file.
The love that might have been
takes shape as the mother of a ghost
sister who instructs the scions in their glory, the ashtray of
cut glass unfolds and is my grandmother
in smug triumph at the mahjong table, hip out of joint
beside the panting angel, the friendships I shed
that collect on my shoulders, epaulettes.
They don't like it, but for us
it's a mercy—joys
and struggles mean everything
they're supposed to mean.

Brasseries & Hedgerows

the brasseries with late-night jams and a soft corner for children
the truant hedgerows and other concessions
that trend wild
                              for now I'm a bitter figure very rich
for writing a book about a dad who goes kon-tiki
and cleans the ocean and the kids kowtow because they can breathe

but I'm a lover that's a phototropic mote in a barn
I banish the ghosts by holding your wrist too tender
for a bar code and follow you inside the museum robot
womb for butterflies, sure the wet unwrapping thoughts
can find the vents and beat the snakeheads in this land

The Raw and the Cooked

It's not that I need to look reasonable,
I say. She carries bags and pets she can't explain
because the boy's leaving home. She feels
undone, as if for some time she was cooked
and now again is raw. Disassembled,
the ingredients lined up in little bowls.
When I come up from the station,
I'll call again and talk you through
the recipe, which is basically wing it
with whatever's in the fridge. The lush
wobbly cobalt portrait of us in the window's
very like the melody that runs along the torqued
rails. I think I can substitute these chords
and so shortly complete the transcription.
I know he'll want to learn it before he leaves.

Madeleine?

Ask why the lost apples
are standing in raw circles
in the snow of whom?
The wooden laughter
seizes the wood
and leaves it, seizes
it but could
you chase down
the mooning
spirit in the well
spots of the forest?
In the meantime
no one comes out
the otherwise ample
house
to smooth my hair.
A pair of finches
pudgy and
contrapuntal is ornament
on the electrical
lines like
rosettes I'm forgetting
on the hem of
whose gown?

Echelons of Spring

Pirates of Lake Champlain

And I know I've no cause to complain,
but let's return to that cove when the waves
are fighting naptime, and the matte black stones
scratch each other on one face, making the same
wiry bearded Dubuffet gnome, the figure
of their guild and watery tinny woodblock
music. Let's each nick two for the sound
in our pockets. Then anywhere we go
the waters that dream of flood and shipwreck
can murmur at us like the very old.
It's not as if without them the voices
of the non-human world would leave us alone.

Melancholy & Spirits

I saw the pale rushes with plumes, the last word
of last year at this threshold where the big
picture windows copied us in black and gold,
disillusioned, hopeful, heartsick, inconsequential.
Walking the frozen deck, making repairs
to the caul of light, you guard us with candles
and blessings of hemlock in the glistering
absent-minded and marauding winds. A knobbly
foal leg, a wedge of cake and—I stubbornly cling
to the mistake overheard in the craving—*pálinka*
pale green flame of clinking spring

I rise like old smoke before dawn

and dressing in the shadow of a penlight, kind of praying
the parquetry complains quietly, is a kind of prayer
in the pale black shirred hush—Let the intricate fish
between me and the family live in the creaking, the kitten and me
naked before some guy with a knack
for playing a normal teacher, I guess, and get

up the shacklike flights to the el like shedding a fond regret,
three gulls posted on the crow-steps, the moon
changing the silvery train to packets of sanctity

the plum paper sky like a scrapbook with pipe smoke
and the plum petal innards of infant smoke and us
the sweet-talk, stuff the city says whenever
it needs to look innocent.

A Little Euthanasia

Those times you turn to me like the moon
in her secret lake, it's lucky I can think,
my deft tongue stiff as hoof: *Can she tell I'm stuck
on the shaft of her light?* I'm on the brink,
hefting the former heavy-weight through the maze of the Loom
Shops where croissant mingles with Febreeze and dander.
We commune with the sweetest loaf of a cat who instructs
us in dignity and pleasure.
The kitchen's raucous in this phase of your grief—
a pregnant hunter,
you're ample with sorrow and laughter;
I taste the silver and furl it at your feet,
amplify the feedback so the void
is on repeat.

Orpheus & Eurydice

The meadows are totally Brooklyn, old drawers
I planted with poppies, as if forensics
boxed her footsteps by flower, and the law's
returned her to her very path, Blahniks
like baubles in her smoking hand. Nearly, eternally
turning from me, footage and message, calamity
on a loop. I don't wish infernal gymnastics
on her but don't exactly mind her cinematic
visits when, sun hissing in the cups of Thalassitis,
she flips off the Mrs. from my green iris.
I pretend she believes that I'm bereft
when I cry out at the cleft where she flickers
in the sunshine. I'm terrified about being left
behind and relishing the terror. What a dick.

All Seats Are Partially Obstructed

I stop in a sort of Bismarck when the dull
dutiful discourse on process and haunch
sandwiches drugs us out of the flow and fall
onto a tableland where the winds launch
a locomotive, a horse that whinnies
and the Orpheus of the age, listening
in his vest, and far away on his sickbed Issa shimmies
upright and says, The scarlet eye inside the starry wings
of the lanternfly is not to be missed.
Suddenly, it just so happens, there, revealed,
the spokes of her bike snip at the fluttery
shadows it is the moon she glides away
the way the spiders spin with maybe a glance at us
changes of the light—believe me, ghost, she's real.

Night in Day

The narrator is irate, the matter
goes nearly as far as July.
But out for a breath on the stoop,
a stretch of song takes root
and blooms inside the lazy-day parade—she's biking by.
The front wheel's the light as seen from a dock,
the back the dicing of the clock.
Strumming the pickets of summer,
aloft on the force of the longing
beaming off your brow,
moonstruck marble, dreaming
of the supple
sculptor who ambles
away for a pint, she's far out ahead of you now.

Book Review (indignant)

A lot of us are talking about her novel,
how real it is, the fracturing
and episodic perceptions, a real
mimesis, I guess, that captures the butterfly
rebirth of a real shit, the artist.
What about the kid, the time of life prop?
Does a prop mimesis blossom into shit junior,
a shooter, a drudge, or through word magic a one-off
of realness despite its crib of unqualities?
I get she wants to hose us down with realness
feelings, but only a real maniac
would perceive her kid as a prop, though as we know
plenty of allegedly real parents are themselves
sketched with a phrase, their best hope in being misread.

The Troubled Sibling

after Sharon Olds

When I look at my younger sister
and she jumps up from behind the lines
in her face, and I feel my knee, the scar on my head
from going first, a miner through a tunnel with few matches,
I want to ask her why she spun me around
and hammered at me and tangled us up in the dark.

These lines coat layers of story so thick
the contour resembles my loneliness.
I can't believe in either of us, though I insist
she saw me see her *genius*, monstrous clarity,
burn the shadows into the past.
At last! I understand. That's how she knows she's
a shadow that the widow, if free
to wander away from the mouth, will not cast.

Collateral Damage

In the audio riptide near
the point of a park the
traffic's like aspen
lather stained in pinks
less flamingo
than innuendo
and notaries on orange bikes
that get your signature
and bike away get it and
bike and at the ivy-covered fountain
in the blind spot of praise
a figure collates
the papers and takes
notes on your disloyal
delight

A Very Dry Man

The seder draws the step-father out of the fine print
of someone's policy, standing, were he a book,
spine to the table, sorry about
the boiler insurance, swaying
in the heat of a candle,
a worn-down selection, dutiful
election that was prefigured
back in Moab when we marched
toward the Great Salt Lake long on the glittering
highway to get gas

as if in that garden of the asperities
the onion produced a pearl
and the pearl could mutter
from the center of obedience
the devotion of the onion

I catch myself mimicking his muttering
like a fish that hopes to comprehend
the history of life on land

Signs of the Death of the Ocean

I went to the plywood
chair to look at the fall two easy
fires were in my head
a punishment from the piece about solitary
a man cherished a match
twice went up in flames and stayed alive on the same page
a poet finds solitude
in swimming laps in my Victorian parlor
again November and the locust feathers
cleave like tongues and patch the asphalt
with bright surrender It's unseemly
to be me The world's unburgeoning
and I want to know if boarding the last transport
to summer's hidden inside the word burgeon

The Yoke

The trees are washed, the trees are blown,
the tiny faces of the fifth grade on Zoom
are hyper-Zeuxian—everything raked,
inflated and riffled, the vacuum-packed
letters of creation set loose and yoked to the verb.
A son shouts his part out the eleventh echelon
of spring! Everything being spoken,
with accents of herb and pollen and *soca*,
bobbing, like the bees at the grapes,
the grateful spoken in the beholden case,
praising for getting to praise inside a home
in the ecstatic disturbed mind of the world.

No need to wake up when the stitching's come loose
a day like this your first companions
slip inside, wind and light printing nervy music
on the bed, you can almost flute it, density
grown holey with the freaking and homing
bird—utter utter thoughts you spring from—ink

I want to get washed in that tattoo
be written on in the original script of the trees
the sign of the gesture that is the trees
and you be scholar of us for the enigma
convinced of the wisdom of the language of my skin

The Coronation of the Ghost

A Very High Fence

Not that long ago, I controlled the territory along the very high fence that defends a remnant of paradise. Unseen hands had snipped the opening in the chain-link at the back of the playground and, riskier, along the road near the convent (the nuns had blue knuckles; each was inexorable), but our feel for the unknown rebels, almost memory, convinced us we were the new guardians. When another gang came into the territory, my forces ran at them and they fled. That unnerved me, but standing on the big rock, watching my toy army scatter the impostors, our doubles—side-lit figures in a nimbus of midges and seed, the fence black against the orange light, valedictory even in victory—standing on the big rock I felt I knew truths that only the big changes could say: the exultation of geese that tack across streams of chapel sunlight, the crepitation of freezing ground, the resignation of sap. How could I teach the others what I sensed when the big changes had been routed as thoroughly as those weaklings?

Almost Like a Call to Come In

The owners of this small town hear tell of hope in self-immolation, go so far as to imagine a slim face growing slimmer and the laughing tip of a cigarette against a blueprint of bodies like basement plumbing, like a human-scale refinery as seen from the turnpike, blue-white stage lights in place of the orange-gray throb. But they're decided in their preference for a light that doesn't harken, just lies there, late morning, some time after the little girls have been paraded up Madison like feather amulets, the little boys a formulating excuse. Visiting up here's like picking up shells in the eye of a storm. At first, every shell's a chip of god, but as you're poured inside the peaceful horn, the biological rock nudges you, peristalsis. Somehow the border's unmarked, and I suspect the elderly on their goat tracks are decoy as from elsewhere I sense a kind of Pinkerton. The pause smells like the glands of an artist. In the secret galleries terra cotta panthers and jade tokens wait for the next age of belief that we'll take to the stars or the roaches oversee, though I wish for the bees in gardens of floral abundance that oxygenate the planet just the way we like it long after we're gone. The best of us, you might have heard, will carry on in such an apiary, but for me the flower shop is plenty, if I remember correctly. Words like *touche* and *davos* are scarcely audible as though already the lopped sacs of the lungs, unpacked from mud, flopped onto a tray, had exhaled. Friends, I also wonder about the flashback, the dive into the nights of the cities in the age of the mechanism, the human form posed against wood and sprockets. Those days are like a pheromone, glory and penumbra, and the answer is chicken empanada with Peruvian green sauce and a blistering-cold IPA.

Book Review (Richard Scarry / anxious)

The ghost that soothes us, you and me both, is an author, let's call him Fox. He wants us to understand that we are ghosts. Thanks, Fox! He points out that the king of the ghosts decreed it: I sign for delivery. He is proven "right," Fox claims, "as surely as seedtime leads to harvest..." What is Fox up to? He blows a mist on stage to soft-focus his crush, we mill about in eons of mellow fruitfulness (to invoke another ghost). In his palm, like a small toad, we go blank so as not to suffer when eaten. It almost works, but through the fog-crochet we see the abandoned tractor out back, not rusted because there's no water. To invoke the seasons in the anthropocene is terrorizing. O, Fox! The growing season is shorter, the pollinators are dying, to say nothing of catastrophic droughts, fires and floods. Will seedtime lead to harvest? Outside ourselves, what certainties are left? The sun, the stars and the moon, gravity, appetite and entropy.

Kafka on the Seesaw

You never meant to split in two, let alone ride a seesaw. Anyway, though it's good, facing yourself, you see some distance over your shoulder into the past and the future, you know those regions will have changed when you gather yourself at the bottom, the present, to spring up, shedding substance in order to attain your very highest height and be crowned king of the ghosts. At the coronation you calibrate the just-left present with the current past and future, gobbling as many changes as can be swallowed and registering with desperate innocence what was or, in the opposite direction, what will be, filling with Big Foots and schemes, dragged down into the present. Once here, you review your domain, but the kingdom is changed in ways that tease you, your claim based on a present you no longer recognize, except it feels like the present, shrinking like the earth for an astronaut escaping the atmosphere, and the past and the future stay remote, even the pity in that, oh, well, you've fallen into the present again, foolish as a lover. And for that, you berate yourself, drugs, mindfulness apps, whiskey flush your contents, you rise again and, again full of nonsense or discernment, fall, you can't be sure your past-facing self is the lord, or is it the bondsman (Wikipedia), and which rightfully (ethically?) deserves the present (both), and you consider jumping off, but who will tend the ghosts?

Crowds and Power

the mass in the pear light gloops through
the portico and oviposits kids in the pews
they combat the taupe and sage noise-suck climate
far back I'm reading the micro-climates the little heads are swaying
in the streaming gossip and turn toward the peppy slideshow
and turn toward the face head
and the unguarded speech of the blind heads sways me
the proto-language of emoto-tropic bulbs
it works on me like the high-toned arches
it works on me like the baroque absence of birds
it works on me like their faith in a slideshow
it works on me like ordination goddamn it

Add It Up

I'm listening to gossip in the lightly
rippling awning like sea lips, the small water lappings
like topographical lapstrake in the low-tide sand
the frivolous lips of the sea that die flapping.
It's the seaside on 3rd, flags and crates of pears
in paper izods, the rare car like a bear
in the shallows. I'm plucking at straws
from the word nest, you might say,
up the fourth of seven
false peaks, next class in ten on 5th,
when it's not that you appear in the gloom of the condo smokestack
that holds in its lap a meager plaza
that holds in its lap a doeskin glove
like one of the green-tan pair you throbbed for in
New Paltz and repented of and yes purchased
not that there and then I remember your fondling the fat
Mont Blanc fountain pen that you frowned at and yes purchased
not that there and then I remember your dreamed-of
waspy pen-name, not that I remember
you said about the Yiddish fellow of whose theater
you were champion his accent embarrassed you
and heaven forefend I see a glove on the bricks like the dregs of a pile
and think *death-camp de Chirico*
or that patted by velvet tentacles from the trees
I'm wrestling this rant about the phony plaza
in the lee of shelves of meat and back and back more stacks of meat
and my strength-sapping dourness.
Not that straws and sparrows slip through the app
when the kiss of a pin-drop invites you in guises
with attendant shades to guide my visit
in the present that gets deleted by the map
or that the inviolable blank photorealist sheen of Madison
offers on a pillow in a Genie's bottle an Ativan and gin
smoothie. But it's not not these things.

36

Latchkey Kid

The sky here's like the Maestro's half-registration
of you on that rock, king of the not wind exactly,
of the afterschool leaf-scuffling escape into the vacant

lot of lots where the worm king, slick as innards
slow as rot, courses the worm-cast world,
where the Maestro might happen to spy you out the mullions

that fly-eye the winter eye whose weight's not nothing
as you weigh the plastic liter corked with a Bounty
wick—you plan to do the things you don't so much know as are

proving to the Maestro, sight-reading the jelly
and cream cheese sky as if fluting at the fretwork stand
in the half-timber study, going steady with a gently bionic woman

a Molotov cocktail can claim, and isn't it like a car
ride, this exquisite boredom, the encouragement of that wastrel
the wind, a long car ride, skipping your soul across

the strip malls, half-dream flickering like your filmy
picture on the glass, the ripping tires that are time going to ground,
the cicada that sloughs its blister-pack skin but not its sound.

Snail Goo, or the Droste Effect

The op-eds on the palindromes inside of us
scatter like the meaning of leaves
and the zelkova that swanlakes

at the window with Mackintosh fanlights
the contralto O that I'd never!
casting the cad's paste gems to the polar shag

and turning, Dutch girl at the gramophone,
with tragical swoons
and the birds! punchy or rabid do they catch rabies? No hope

in getting your bearings
from this bunch, no one else to get them
from, and still the wish to be less, um, agog

not flighty but feathered
heir to the songbird, not the frog-
fucking chimp. To be no less

than wish litter
on the moss and meal,
crumbs of if and else

the Algorithm will happen on:
"I made this garden.
I didn't know you were in here!"

What's Bad

Not living in Mexico
and reading about the new Mexican thriller
they're confiscating at the border

Leaving your phone in the kitchen
and not your friends or the gorgeous bartender being able to unglue

Having an idea
that you can't support with reference to court decisions
the way the lawyers do

Having traded small caresses with your wife throughout the day
and making room in bed for your son who's had a nightmare

Not thinking of yourself as part of the team
but the members insisting
you have to belong to something

Seeing your dear departed father
in the mirror

Very bad:
Your store of twilight safran
drying out in the Cloud
without a pinch of irony

And worst of all:
Dying in the Late Anthropocene
the graveyard washed out
power down no way to complete the cremation

The Snackbar on the Alp of the Mind

On First Looking into *A Defence of Poetry*

I got bored pretty quick and wandered o'er bracken
into a cabin with cardinal windows and static air,
for there, as legislator, I'd dodge the jealous
gods coming up the hill. Ever vigilant, sometimes
I get distracted by the fire. I'm the ashes of the net
the future will read, the salmon and the stream
and this wasp, crisp little chap, light-fucked
at the sugar pane, and mom's kidney transplant, mixing
self with self, as on the B103
at the mannequin hour, assembled
and separate, and so you part
with me and repair, like the accordion
bus, singing a little, come on up to the house
for now, you're safe, for now

What Keyhole of Instructive Light

You say seaside because you see
the light on the blufflike projects
with pinks on the gestures in the sky and violets
in their decay, lemon on the pasteboard steeple and seagulls
that cry arcs over the syrups and refugees my son the same
ocean open notebook I wonder of

The Snackbar on the Alp of the Mind

I number among the good in this lobe
half into my jacket, buttering my toast
and the pure butter's delighted with itself
and the toast is touting its humble smell
when the dog wanders in from an anecdote
about the joy of the dog and the germaphobe:
The kids were stealing coasters. They were hiding under the table
when who should wander in? You guessed it—Mable,
talking about the time it was the Pope she cured
or somebody like him—it may be the Pope's sure,
but he's not here,
though I hear
he's a toast connoisseur.
Not to say he's disapproving.
With a caboose like that he's got to be grooving.
Care to flicker between meadow and kitchen like a strobe?
I number among the good in this lobe.
I number among the good in this lobe.

unbound books
vols. 6, 9, & 14

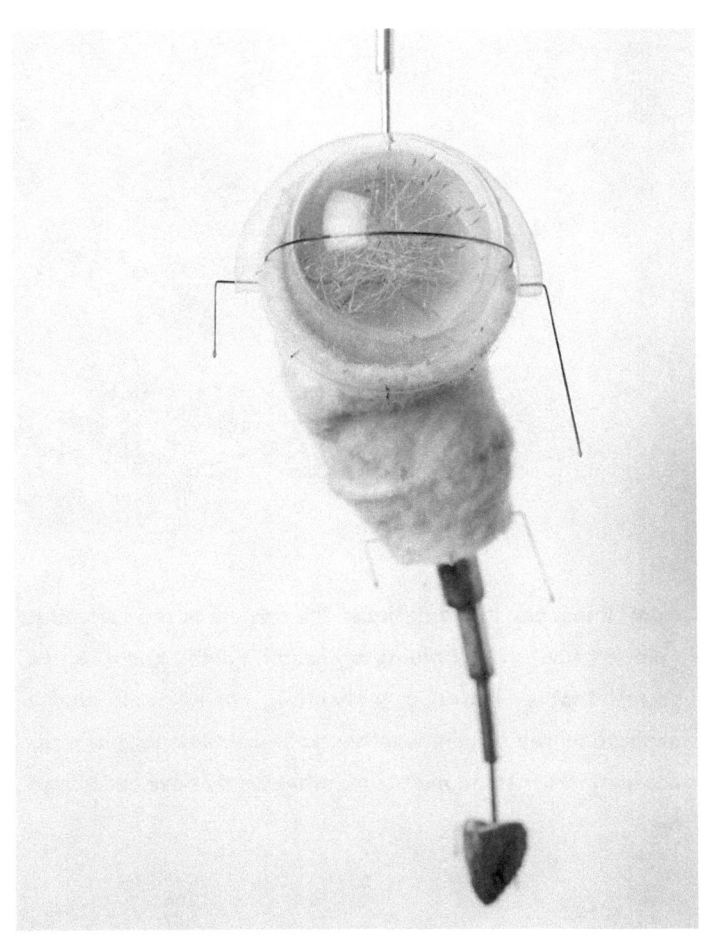

The Romance of the Fittest

Now I know you heard desire in the corners of my voice, but I didn't know I wasn't hiding my secret, I didn't know I had a secret, that I wanted a connection, craved it so that I exposed myself to your weather, your instruments. If not for the instincts that led me to you, what would have become of me?

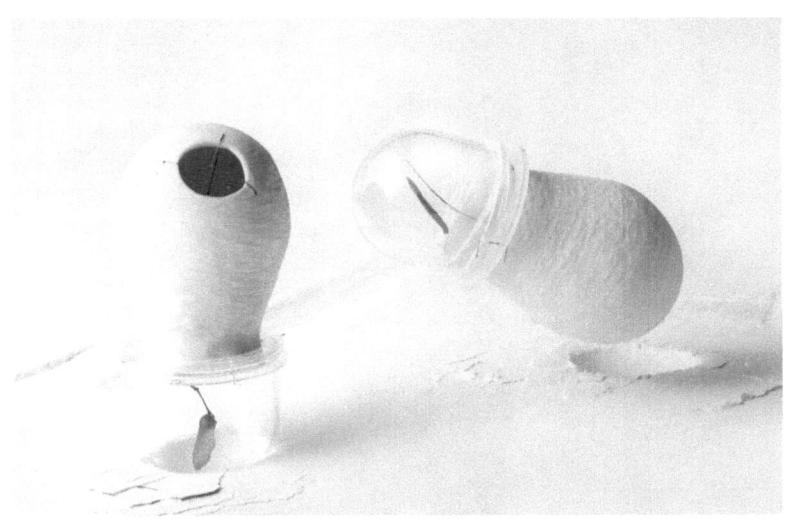

Near the bridge over the oxbow, an oriole was building a nest. We never would've touched it, of course, but the maple sent a helicopter to us, you said, a token that traveled a surprising distance over the field and water so that we could vamoose and remember the nest, the forest protecting its people, you said. Protecting us, too, I said, with a token against hardness, an invitation to return to the forest, to a degree, you said, yes. It makes you think about objects and memories, doesn't it? In shaping us, wherein lies the difference?

51

We'll call again when we arrive, should be pretty soon, but your mother's hungry — we need to find a diner or something — and your father misses you — he's been musing, with that fond look he gets, I assume, can't really see him but that's how he sounds. Love you.

Rendez-Vous
with the
Revelator

In which a barber (& amateur herpetologist), who departed this plane in 189–, transmits messages on the frequency of artifacts made by Michael Aaron Lee, impersonating an art critic and instructing us in heretofore unrecorded ideas about the avocado & c.

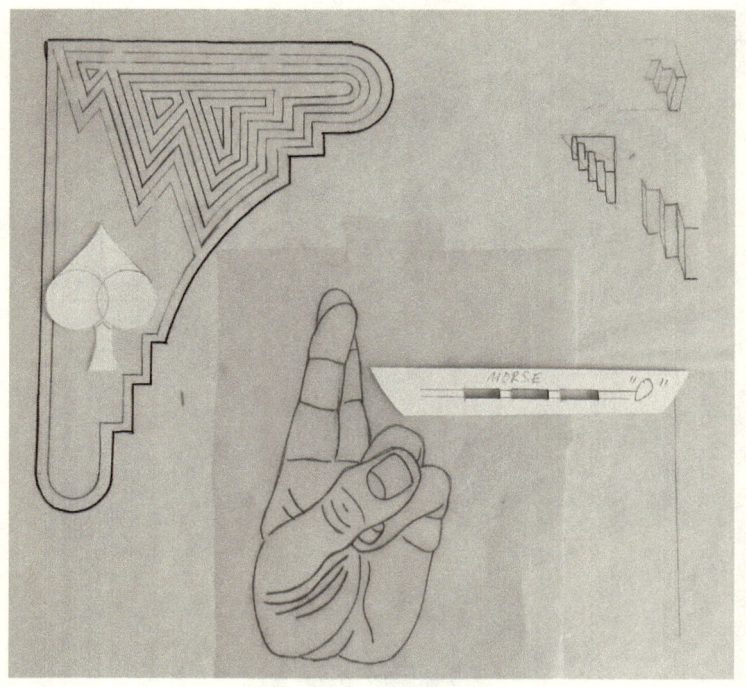

I am a learned and toothless ex-barber of the post-blood-letting, pre-antibiotics school, a lubricator of dirty gears through commerce in tinctures and card games. A *soi-disant* so to speak **avocado**, guac-ripe with the wisdom that can only come of storing at center a considerable pit. Picture me in the unpaved street of my Wisconsin town. Something like a candy apple, something like Baudelaire in his smock and Boho bowtie. That's not me! I am approaching you but haven't arrived yet. You're getting the flavor – penny sewn into the hem of taffeta skirt.

Michael Aaron Lee's work evokes the age of the traveling huckster, when the blood stains in the parlor went unremarked and mass somnambulism was achieved with hats, corsets, varnish, and a whimpering lamplight that promoted congress with ghosts. A sped-up time-lapse film of Lee's process would render idiosyncratic rhythms that oppose the factory mesmerism a person might expect of the sawtooth, gearlike layers in the finished pieces, layers that might otherwise seem to grow crystal-like out of the grid on which the works are planned. But at the same time, the not dreamed of in your philosophy Horatio reality that illusion represents is actualized in Lee's works. Sure, the stepwise motion cuts against illusion, grit in the emollient of avocado theory, which would *lumpens* the social atoms, i.e., you and you. Here it's worth involving Zaha Hadid, who, *mutatis mutandis*, encodes orthography's threat to the comprehension of boundaries in her ossographic architecture, which can be called *concrete* or *literalist* for conducting us in crossing thought borders just as Lee's artifacts — sketch; collage; x-acto scraps; shimmed, glued, graphite-rich constructions that gleam soberly — enact the transmigration of souls. Yes, Lee is that rare thing, an honest medium. Is he wary? He has nothing to fear from me, but the others don't play.

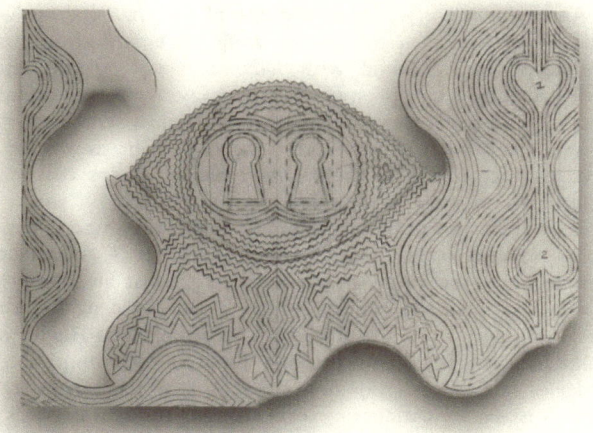

Working my way along a process that can only ever be partial, I don't have great odds of materializing in my entirety, but then you know what that's like. Thing is, don't worry about any of us – despite my father's predictions, I surely did right in dedicating myself to avocado theory.

The **ripe** avocado can slip through the keyhole as abstraction – mother, desire, penis, snake, truth. Whichever you in your innocence need, in that fashion I escape, with a wet squeak, bumpy reddish lozenges and, alone at last, the whirr of your machinery.

Sparrows

Mr. Met had scooped the clamor with an orange
net and stowed it in the scaffolding,
a cratch of sparrows in a white brick alcove
on East 94th. The lack of gravel for hopping
and picking in isn't audible
in this recording in which you find yourself
a chorus.

57

Someone called the electrostatic trees
out of the skies of the clouds of cement. They took
green root in the kitchen.
I'd stopped at H Mart. It was the simmering
japchae dumplings that, small and smaller,
chirped in the pan.

Unusually on the A the shrunken trees
chirped into leaf — it was the chrome double
doors, perfectly not true,
rubbing in the channel like gladness in a chance
sunbeam.

Mind the Gap

It's Raining

stunt doubles for the hands that touched you and the number
you wish had touched you raised to the power of oblivion

those spirits now clerks in the office of the clarities
that register the obstructions (slates bikes us) until the clay is washed away

machinery of softest redress
like the girl who listens in the branches of the poem

the verb of thingness in the abandoned mood
the camouflage that makes anyone into a search party

the rain's a small country with no phone

Mind the Gap

"I have grown accustomed to the fact that the world here is wrecked in the morning and blooms again in the evening."

"And when the day reaches its end I hear the crickets and become entirely full and unintelligible."

"Mom!"

"They're in the kitchen."

Public Private Partnership

I'd stay with the giant who knocks
the lanternfly
off his big sunny
bald crown and says No
and His bad
luck to land on my head
after I stamp on it. I'd say
sorry as I coaxed its cousin
or mother to eat sugar
off my shoulder.
The tide's out on the day.
He drifts on
up the block where a few
new executioners
are listing far out
on the broad bright sidewalk,
twos and threes on lunch
break touching
under the Opera
House marquee, others
trickling across the whale-
back of the road, #trickbikes
@wholefoods on the shimmering
plaza. He moves
among the hunted
creatures that star
the rim of his morning
glory trash can
with a heavyweight's very
small feints, guiding them over
the cracks, casually
mindful, ceremonious
and clear
like the sky.

It was hard to leave you in the bed
but I slipped out when the clouds slid in

snuck up on the shore
between a gleam and a glint

and with the last green leaf
skimmed a cup of lake

spread it across my questions like a web
and tuned the concept well past moonlight

then put it to the scoop of your hip
to listen for the qualia of your skin.

Something like the sibilant wisdom
we grant to photons on their headlong chase

clarified the blunders of the human race—
in the probable joy of strings and branes

I scraped the bottomlessness of the fiction
of person in which roadhouse a nowhere sax

convinced me again of the gutbucket basis
of your faces.

Anderson on the Porch

for Nils

Slung over the lumber chair just looking
at the lumpen low mountains lazy
with the names of those shapes
and arranging them a little

with the blotches that shift the woods—
the pod of buttered pencil-white clouds
throws down hush on the clamoring
coquettish and acquisitive greens
fragile as a newt's hand or son

of fractal, up close and far, leaves to trees
to woods, the wooded mounds to the clouds
prod ginger Anderson to shape each arrangement
and arrange each shape by grander sun-
set so to speak as iteration is to isotope when a red

feint reminds him of the chamber
in the pines
he thinks he knew
if not a pertness
a vigilance
like an arch *bouquiniste*
from whose shelf-lined cabinet
the cardinal, fussing, festoons
the field in red knife

and not a lick less dull over the lakelike pool
the swallows, like snippets of horseplay from out back
of a barn where the women repair the land or some
earth-moving machinery—each
woman world and window—and stir
hoppy ale in scintillant pots,
weave symbols in the soft loose hair of the day

March

It's April on the train.
We just played
in the tropical parlors at the Hockney
after puking in the doctor's lobby.
It wasn't so much the bloodwork as the anticipation,
like the antlike delegation
that crawls up the Dutch dream of a mountain spine in shrinking file,
donkeys, monks and soldiers that *tick*
tick tick around the treelike lobstery fountain and peristyle
while in the central panel I'm in the grip
of the shameless curiosity
of that old baby
who seems about to say something hard, like *Saskatchewan*,
but without breaking eye contact latches on.
It's a little much, you're right.
I like to think
that in the third panel you return to the Frick
and are replete with *The Polish Rider*'s punk assumption of the light.
Being
this guy without you is like seeing
an adult with shoes on the wrong feet.
Really, really, you thought we wouldn't meet?
On the 6 the kids snatch at the dazzle—
banners, screens, jade and periwinkle
seats, the gleaming chrome, like ornamentation
in the AI nation
parade. The spirit of disco has blessed the caboose—
everybody's loose,
grooving on a bright-saudade escape-
artist duo,
the rangy one in Pepto
bob, lemon jacket

and sugary culottes,
the fireplug in a kelly bycocket
with mohair cape.
The kids pole-dance and strike a pose
beside the comicstrip sweethearts
with meadowfresh vogue.
If I were a painter,
I'd use Hockney's palette.
You'd be worked through the scene as a tremor.
Will you bother
to see—
preacher, poet, tzaddik, churro vendor,
fistfuls of hollyhocks,
fat tears of bok
choy, a ghost-loosening loop
of ghostly bossa,
one polka dot backpack with a placid lhasa
apso,
six hands sticky with soap—
bother to see me
here?
This painting doesn't fear
the critic, the background is the playground, near
to Sinai where fire,
ladybug and Godzilla boots write
midrash in the snow like a minuscule tag
on a grain of rice.
I don't like to brag
about the kids. Suffice
it to say the sight-lines converge
on them, too, and now that I know about emergent
properties, such as the sense
that I am insofar as I'm under surveillance,
in the cold universe
it's good to be watched by doctors and not worse

to be pinged at by the orbiting string
of pearls because you *know* you're the girl in her turning,
shedding fomo
and pity like Mrs Clark, née Birtwell of Soho,
toes in the shag,
all but saying, What a drag
to have been the beloved, like standing in your own hair.
To have been stripped by you, Alistair.
This picture unfolds *ad infinitum*,
and though the kids hoped
they'd get to keep the friendly jackalopes—
they wanted to invite them
for dinner—
that pair of joyous sinners,
now smaller than a point, makes like a leaf
at Spring Street.

NOTES

"Come On Up to the House" is the title of a song by Tom Waits.

"Sheila" is the title of a song by Morphine.

"Misterioso" is the title of a song by Thelonious Monk.

"The Troubled Sibling" is inspired by "The Elder Sister" by Sharon Olds.

"Almost Like a Call to Come In" takes its title from "Come In" by Robert Frost.

"Snail Goo, or The Droste Effect" recasts Raven's remark on meeting the first human, as told in "Pea-Pod Man" by Virginia Hamilton in *In the Beginning*.

In "Book Review (Richard Scarry / anxious)," I put a copy of Tom Hennen's toad ("Another Toad") and quote *Fragments of an Infinite Memory: My Life with the Internet* by Maël Renouard.

"Add It Up" is the title of a song by Violent Femmes.

"What's Bad" imitates "What's Bad" by Gottfried Benn, translated by Michael Hoffmann.

"What Keyhole of Instructive Light" is influenced by "Dark Corner" by Alfred Starr Hamilton.

"Mind the Gap" puts two statements in dialogue or at least the same room. A. B. Yehoshua wrote the first in a letter to Bernard Avishai, quoted in Avishai's "A. B. Yehoshua's Culture War" in *Tablet Magazine*, September 9, 2022. The second is from *Água Viva* by Clarice Lispector, translated by Stefan Tobler.

"It's Raining" is inspired by "It's Raining" by Guillaume Apollinaire.

"Public Private Partnership," especially the final cadence, is influenced by Charles Bukowski's "No. 6."

73

ACKNOWLEDGMENTS

Many thanks to the editors and staff of the following journals for publishing versions of these poems:

DIAGRAM—"It was hard to leave you in the bed," "A Little Euthanasia," and "Add It Up" (with a different title)

Rhino—"It's Raining"

Cobra Milk—"Signs of the Death of the Ocean"

Matter—"Almost Like a Call to Come In" (with a different title), "Crowds and Power," "A Very High Fence," and "What's Bad"

Nu Review—"Bushwick Yellow," "Sheila," "Misterioso," "In the porches of the ear," "What Did You Think It Was About," "Brasseries & Hedgerows," "The Raw and the Cooked," "I rise like old smoke before dawn," "Book Review (indignant)," "A Very Dry Man," "Book Review (Richard Scarry / anxious)," "Snail Goo, or The Droste Effect" and "Mind the Gap"

The Saint Ann's Review—"No need to wake up when the stitching's come loose"

Sporklet—"Madeleine?," "On First Looking into *A Defence of Poetry*," and "What Keyhole of Instructive Light"

I'm grateful to Dr. Ross Tangedal, Grace Dahl, Kylie Newton, Elyse Edens, Carolyn Czerwinski, and the entire staff of Cornerstone Press for making this beautiful book.

I'm grateful to the friends who read drafts of many of these poems: Nils Folke Anderson, Jane Avrich, Peter Cole, Jordan Davis, Doug Fishbone, Rajiv Gulati, David Pauley, Karen Russo, Kikki Short, and Matt Sosnow. I need to spotlight polymath Michael Pershan, who played a net game, returning shanks with inexhaustible enthusiasm and interesting spin. Thanks to Virginia Konchan for her discernment and encouragement. For entrusting me with their work for a venture in the gift economy, unbound books, thanks to Nils Folke Anderson, Rosaire Appel, Paul Benney, Beth Bosworth, Jordan Davis, Virginia Konchan, Michael Aaron Lee, Peter Myers, Alexis Myre, Jeffrey Joe Nelson, D. Nurkse, Matthew Rohrer, Marty Skoble, Glenn Shaheen, and Sandor Weiner. And thanks to Nils and Alexis for opening up their gallery, Nightshift, to unbound books.

*

Melissa Kantor, without whom not

BENJAMIN GANTCHER is a Pushcart Prize nominee and the recipient of a LABA fellowship as well as residencies from the UCross Foundation and the Omi International Arts Center. He is the author of the poetry collection *Snow Farmer* (2017), a finalist in several contests, and the poetry chapbook *Strings of Math and Custom* (2013). Gantcher's first poetry manuscript, *If a Lettuce*, earned finalist honors in the National Poetry Series and Bright Hill Press contests. His poems and essays have appeared in many journals, including *Tin House, Slate, Rhino, Guernica, The Brooklyn Rail,* and *DIAGRAM*. Gantcher was Poet of the Week at Brooklyn Poets and is a former poetry editor of *failbetter*.

He is the editor, publisher and designer of unbound books, "free, downloadable, printable, foldable, downright handsome books," that can be found @benjamingantcher, at the unbound books Substack, and at https://gantcher.wordpress.com/unbound-books/.